12·11·01

P9-CLS-327

Written by Cari Meister

Illustrated by Terry Sirrell

Children's Press®
A Division of Grolier Publishing
New York • London • Hong Kong • Sydney
Danbury, Connecticut

For John, who loves the biggest rocks best of all.
—C. M.

For my 3½-year-old daughter, Flynn,
who said to me while I illustrated this book,
"This is for you, Daddy," and handed me a rock.
—T. S.

Reading Consultants
Linda Cornwell
Coordinator of School Quality and Professional Improvement
(Indiana State Teachers Association)

Katharine A. Kane
Education Consultant
(Retired, San Diego County Office of Education
and San Diego State University)

Visit Children's Press® on the Internet at:
http://publishing.grolier.com

Library of Congress Cataloging-in-Publication Data
Meister, Cari.
  I love rocks / by Cari Meister ; illustrated by Terry Sirrell.
      p. cm. — (Rookie reader)
Summary: A child rhapsodizes about rocks from big to small and precious to commonplace.
  ISBN 0-516-22152-3 (lib. bdg.)   0-516-27293-4 (pbk.)
  [1. Rocks—Fiction. 2. Stories in rhyme.] I. Sirrell, Terry ill. II. Title. III. Series.
PZ8.3.M5514 II 2001
[E]—dc21   00-030698

Rocks, rocks, rocks!

3

I love rocks!

4

5

Some are heavy.
Some are light.

Some are black.

8

Some are white.

Some are round.
Some are square.
Some have freckles.
Some have hair!

Some float.

Some sink.

13

Some are slimy.
Some stink!

15

Rocks, rocks, rocks!
I love rocks!

They make castles.

They make caves.

They make dams.

They make churches.
They make graves.

21

They make glass.

They make pools.

They are big, like mountains.

They make jewels.

They cover the earth.
They fit in my hand.

They are small, like sand.

Word List (40 Words)

are	float	jewels	sand
big	freckles	light	sink
black	glass	like	slimy
castles	graves	love	small
caves	hair	make	some
churches	hand	mountains	square
cover	have	my	stink
dams	heavy	pools	the
earth	I	rocks	they
fit	in	round	white

About the Author

Cari Meister lives on a small farm in Minnesota with her husband John, their dog Samson, two horses, three cats, two pigs, and two goats. She is the author of more than twenty books for children, including *Catch That Cat!* (also a Rookie Reader), *When Tiny Was Tiny,* and *Busy, Busy City Street* (both from Viking).

About the Illustrator

Terry Sirrell has been a cartoonist and illustrator since 1983. His cartoons and characters have appeared on the backs of cereal boxes, in the advertising of numerous major corporations, and in dozens of publications. Terry also illustrates children's books, greeting cards, and jigsaw puzzles.

Rocks, rocks, rocks!
I love rocks!

31